Claim Your Light

Gaining Insight For A Fulfilling Life

Wayne Benenson, Ph.D

Barb Hughson, Ed.D

Copyright © 2017@GreatMasters, Inc.

Claim Your Light – Gaining Insight for a Fulfilling Life Workbook

© Copyright 2017, GreatMasters, Inc., Dr. Wayne Benenson and Dr. Barb Hughson

All rights reserved.

ISBN: 978-0-9985656-0-6

No part of this book may be reproduced, stored in a retrieval system, or transmitted in any form or by any means, electronic, mechanical, photocopying, recording, or by any information retrieval system, or otherwise without the prior express written consent of the authors, except for the inclusion of brief quotations in critical articles or a review.

This workbook is a supplement to the *'Claim Your Light'* workshop, the book, and the online curriculum. It is designed to help you deal with uncertainty in your life and to further the unfathomably deep connection to your greatness. Take time to be introspective and ask the tough questions to reach that depth. The activities in this workbook will help you understand the fears and discomfort associated with those questions. This process of reflection can help you grow into the vibrant person you already are. Your greatness has always been present, however it may not have always been conscious. This may have created an illusion that you are looking at your life from the wings, waiting for your entrance. The activities in this workbook can sharpen your focus and remind you of your connection to your deepest and most authentic self. It is time for your moment on center stage. See yourself there. See yourself there. Use this workbook to help you get there. When you get there drop us a line on our website (http://www.greatmastersinc.com/) and tell us how it feels.

Dr. Wayne & Dr. Barb

Chapter 1

Introduction: Outer Wholeness + Inner Quiet = Hidden Vitality

1. Self-awareness is a first step to shifting your energy and increasing emotional intelligence. Describe a situation where you reacted in a way that was not effective or creative. Describe what you were thinking. How were you feeling?

_____

_____

_____

_____

_____

_____

_____

_____

_____

_____

2. Self-awareness is a conscious knowledge of one's own character, feelings, motives, and desires. Jot down some initial thoughts on how you can improve your self-awareness and expression of your emotions?

_____

_____

_____

_____

_____

_____

_____

_____

_____

_____

_____

_____

_____

3. Rate yourself on these conditions which can lead to increased awareness. Describe your behavior by circling the appropriate number from the following code:

5 = very present in my regular behavior
4 = somewhat present n my regular behavior
3 = neutral or no opinion
2 = hardly present in my regular behavior
1 = rarely present in my regular behavior

1 2 3 4 5

1. FLEXIBILITY – can generate many different ideas rapidly

1 2 3 4 5

2. TOLERANCE OF AMBIGUITY – comfort in situations where everything is not in order

1 2 3 4 5

3. SPONTANEITY – responding to situations directly rather than following someone else's plan

1 2 3 4 5

4. ADVENTUROUSNESS – a love of exploring the world around you and exploring the inner self

1 2 3 4 5

5. BOLDNESS – acting confidently and humbly if opinions re challenged

4. Given your rating in # 3, in which areas would you give priority to increase and sustain your self-awareness? Why?

5. Envision a new way to manage and control your emotions. Change the caption of the cartoon below to reflect your top priority to manage your emotions.

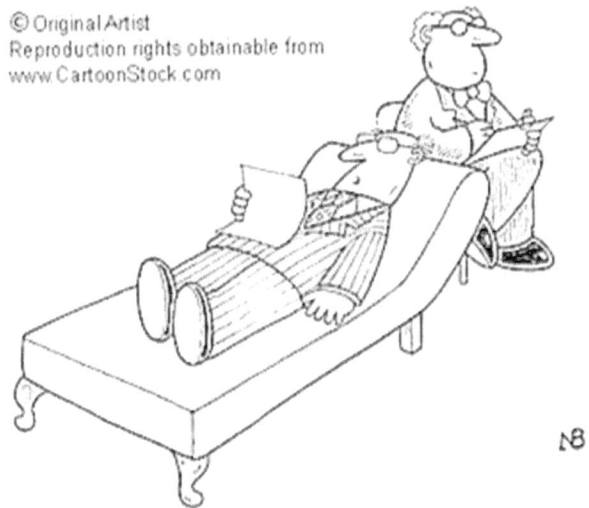

"Agenda item 1 : My obsessive need to control"

"Agenda item 1: My need to _____"

6. List 3 intentions you can set for yourself at the start of each day to bring you to a place of heightened self-awareness.

1. _____
   _____
   _____

Claim Your Light - Gaining Insight for a Fulfilling Life Workbook

2. _____

3. _____

7. Who can you enlist to help you provide observations of how they experience you expressing and managing your emotions?

_____
_____
_____
_____
_____
_____
_____
_____

Chapter 2

Home Plate – Identifying Our Needs

1. Reflect on a current situation that is a challenge for you. Is this challenge a high concern? What is the unexpressed need?

   _____

   _____

   _____

   _____

   _____

   _____

   _____

   _____

   _____

   _____

   _____

   _____

2. Think about some of the reasons why this need is not being met? What parts can you change? What parts can't you change?

_____

_____

_____

_____

_____

_____

_____

_____

_____

_____

_____

_____

_____

_____

_____

3. Think about a time from your past when you were dealing with a challenging (or seemingly impossible) situation. How did you resolve the problem? Or, alternatively, think about someone you know who has dealt with a challenging situation. How did she or he resolve the problem?

_____

_____

_____

_____

_____

_____

_____

_____

_____

_____

_____

_____

_____

4. What would your life look like if your need was met and the challenge was no longer an issue? Sketch out an image of the new look to your life.

A. Complete the following:

❖ In order for my specific need to be met, (briefly state your need)

_____

_____

_____

here's what I will do:

_____

_____

_____

by this date:

_____

_____

_____

❖ When I fall off the wagon in completing my plan to meet this need I will do these three things:

(an action, perhaps a smaller task, I know I can complete)

1. _____
   _____
   _____

(a feeling or affirmation that rewards honest effort, especially during stressful moments)

2. _____
   _____
   _____

(a reach out to my "helper buddy" and say):

3. _____
   _____
   _____

Chapter 3

First Base – Empathy: Caring About Others To Promote Self-Care

1. Describe someone you know (or someone from history) who you believe exhibits great empathy. What personal qualities define empathy?

   _____

   _____

   _____

   _____

   _____

   _____

2. The suffix *-pathy* means "feeling" or "suffering." The prefix *em-* means "within" or "inside." So, *empathy* is the ability to understand and share the feelings of another. The prefix *a-* means "not" or "without." So, *apathy* is a lack of interest, enthusiasm, or concern. To have the *most* possible empathy (and therefore the least possible apathy) means you feel the feelings of another with the greatest accuracy and effort. On the other hand, to have the most possible apathy (and the *least* possible empathy) means you no accuracy in feeling the feelings of another, or simply, you not try at all. Both empathy

and apathy are contagious, that is, they spread from one person to another by direct or indirect contact.

Recount a story of the empathy – apathy continuum. Perhaps you showed empathy toward a co-worker who was experiencing a distressing situation, in an office culture that shunned negative or conflictual expressions of feelings. Were the empathy apathy responses contagious? On a continuum of 1 to 10 with 1 being "High Empathy" and 10 being "High Apathy," what number was your feeling toward the co-worker? What feeling were most other workers in the office to the co-worker? Was it hard to find common ground? Why or why not?

_____

_____

_____

_____

_____

_____

3. Use the case study above to discuss the perspectives of other parties. What number would you give them on the Empathy-Apathy continuum? Why?

Your co-worker friend — ___

_____

_____

_____

A co-worker quite uncomfortable with her position — ___

_____

_____

_____

A co-worker somewhat uncomfortable with her position— ___

_____

_____

_____

Your boss' reaction to her position — ___

_____

_____

_____

How might this perspective sharing exercise shift your attitude about how to practice compassion in a conflictual environment?

_____

_____

_____

_____

_____

4. Tell about an incident where you practiced "radical listening" (You let people have their say, held back from interrupting and reflected back what they told you so they knew you were really listening.)

___
___
___
___
___
___
___
___
___
___
___
___
___
___
___
___

5. Timing and sincerity are so important in demonstrating empathy. Explain a personal encounter when a mistimed remark or a perception of not really caring caused your empathetic response to blow up in your face. Do you relate to the cartoon below? How?

_____
_____
_____
_____
_____
_____
_____
_____
_____
_____
_____
_____
_____
_____

EMPATHY

6. Describe a situation where you showed empathy? What motivated you to extend yourself to another person (or animal) without any thought of compensation?

_____

_____

_____

_____

_____

_____

_____

_____

_____

_____

Chapter 4

Second Base – Grit: Persistence in Spite of the Obstacles

1. Two Greek words connote different notions of time. *Chronos* time refers to chronological or sequential time, as in "I have a doctor's appointment at 2:00 pm." *Kairos* time signifies a time lapse, a moment of indeterminate time in which everything happens; the right or opportune moment (the supreme moment), as in "I was working on my stamp collection and totally lost track of time."

Describe a situation where you were operating in *Kairos* time. What made this time special? Did your activity tap strong passion within you? How did you feel?

_____

_____

_____

_____

_____

_____

_____

_____

_____

2. Rate yourself on these grit attributes. Circle the most accurate descriptor to these questions:

   a. Do you believe that effort beats talent?

   ALWAYS   MOST OF THE TIME   SOMETIMES   NEVER

   b. Do you believe that deliberate practice can increase resilience?

   ALWAYS   MOST OF THE TIME   SOMETIMES   NEVER

   c. Do you believe that grit is a learnable skill?

   ALWAYS   MOST OF THE TIME   SOMETIMES   NEVER

   d. Do you believe that moving from "commandment" mentality (victim thinking) to "commitment" mindset (creative thinking) can release restrictive beliefs?

   ALWAYS   MOST OF THE TIME   SOMETIMES   NEVER

   e. In dealing with failure or rejection when you fall down, can you accept "what is," rather than the story you tell yourself by which you interpret your circumstance?

   ALWAYS   MOST OF THE TIME   SOMETIMES   NEVER

   f. Can you be kind to yourself during the process of change?

   ALWAYS   MOST OF THE TIME   SOMETIMES   NEVER

3. The law of attraction is a belief that the magnetic power of the Universe draws similar energies together. It manifests through the power of creation, everywhere and in many ways. This law attracts <u>to you</u> the thoughts, ideas, people, situations and circumstances of a similar kind. It is the law and power that brings together people of similar interests, who unite into various groups, such as political groups, sports teams, sports fans, fraternities, etc.

   a. How much do you identify with this belief? Circle the most accurate descriptor to this question:

   Do I believe in the Law of Attraction?

   ALWAYS   MOST OF THE TIME   SOMETIMES   NEVER

   b. If you are open to broadening your belief that positive thoughts are magnets for positive life experiences, there are several thing you can do. You can take advantage of this law through creative *visualization* and *affirmations*. By visualizing a mental image of what you want to achieve or by repeating positive statements, which are called affirmations, you create and bring into your life what you visualize or repeat in your mind. In other words, you use the power of your mind, thoughts, imagination and words to help fulfill specific desires.

Claim Your Light - Gaining Insight for a Fulfilling Life Workbook

Bring to mind your problem (see chapter 2, number 1). Jot down two images of *creative visualization* that will help you focus joyfully on that desire:

_____

_____

_____

_____

_____

_____

_____

Bring to mind your problem (see chapter 2, number 1). Jot down two *affirmations* that will help you focus joyfully on that desire:

_____

_____

_____

_____

_____

_____

_____

4. Describe a time in your own life when you used grit to reach a goal. Was that situation unique or familiar? When you reflect upon it, was this an easy reach for the goal or did you really have to dig deep, and if so, how did you do that?

_____
_____
_____
_____
_____
_____
_____
_____
_____
_____
_____
_____
_____
_____
_____
_____
_____
_____

5. To avoid extreme peaks or valleys which can paralyze action, GreatMasters advocates a *both/and* approach to problem solving. Therefore, "change" is paired with its opposite, "stability." Complete the T-graph below using a *both/and* response to a current unresolved problem

   a. Describe in a few words the nature of your unresolved problem (for example: relationship issue, money issue, health issue, etc.):

   _____

   _____

   _____

   _____

   _____

   _____

   b. Now fill in the "Advantages" and "Disadvantages" associated with this Change / Stability response.

CHANGE	**STABLE**
What happens if I allow a change?	What happens if I do not allow change?

ADVANTAGES _____

_____

_____

_____

_____

DISADVANTAGES _____

c. In going forward, what is acceptable to me so I can manage change differently?

Chapter 5

Third Base – Growth Mindset: Facing Challenges By Learning From Our Mistakes

1. **A Fixed Mindset (FM)** is a belief that intelligence is set for life. Therefore all effort is geared to upholding an image of being smart or looking good. When obstacles occur, any negative feedback is seen as threatening. This results in achieving less, giving up easily and believing in a fatalistic view of life.

   A Growth Mindset (GM) is a belief that intelligence is fluid and can be developed. Effort is the key to mastery and persistence in the face of setbacks. Feedback, positive or negative, is seen as a way to learn which results in reaching higher levels of achievement and a greater sense of free will.

In the blank before each of the following descriptions write **FM** if the behavior or belief represents a Fixed Mindset or **GM** if the behavior or belief represents a Growth Mindset.*

a. _____ It's a dog-eat-dog world. If I don't protect myself, who will?

b. _____ When in doubt, it's important to show a sign of strength.

c. _____ Talent can be developed through effort and seeking help from others.

d. _____ Working your hardest means establishing your superiority.

e. _____ Working your hardest means doing and becoming your best.

f. _____ In a conflict, point out the obstacles created by the other person.

g. _____ In a conflict, the problem comes from fixed traits, it can't be solved.

h. _____ In a conflict, acknowledge one's partners imperfections without assigning blame.

i. _____ In a conflict, the problem is of communication, not personality or character.

2. Think of a past success in which you reached a particular goal or milestone in your life. Give a short answer response to each question below:

   a. Describe the goal or milestone.

   _____

   _____

   b. What caused you to persevere?

   _____

   _____

   c. What did you value most that sustained you?

   _____

   _____

d. Did your ability and confidence grow with your effort?

___

e. Would you have changed your effort in any way? Why or why not?

___
___
___
___
___
___
___
___
___

3. Think of a mistake you made recently. What were your thoughts or feelings before others became aware of what happened? What did you do after the mistake became known?

___
___
___
___

Claim Your Light - Gaining Insight for a Fulfilling Life Workbook

_____

_____

_____

4. a. Describe a situation where you used feedback, both positive and negative, in a productive way?

_____

_____

_____

_____

_____

_____

_____

_____

_____

b. Describe a situation where you used feedback, either positive or negative, in an unproductive way?

_____

_____

_____

_____

_____

_____

c. Compare these stories. How might you use feedback as a means for growth? Can risking making a mistake help you find new strategies and behaviors to solve a problem?

5. Compare these two praise statements. Which do you think would be more effective? Why?

- "Great effort. You tried your best."
- "A good first try. This is new information for you. How can you use it for the next step?"

6. Share a personal story about a time you had to work hard to get better at something. In this struggle story include specific examples of:

- Hard work
- Strategies to overcome obstacles
- Seeking help from others.

_____

_____

Claim Your Light - Gaining Insight for a Fulfilling Life Workbook

_____

_____

_____

_____

_____

_____

_____

_____

_____

* *Answers for number 1: GM for c, e, h, i.*

Chapter 6

Getting to Home Plate: Living With Our Questions

1. What is one of my goals that I never seem to reach (losing weight, changing jobs, financial independence, etc.)?

   _____

   a. Although you've encountered setback in reaching your goal, do you believe parts of the Key 3 (empathy, grit, growth mindset) can get you closer to your goal this time?

   YES   NO

   b. Are you willing to ask yourself the tough questions to increase your learning capacity?

   YES   NO

   c. Are you willing (at least in your mind's eye) to be open-minded and open-hearted on the journey to a more competent and confident you?

   YES   NO

   d. Are you willing to be more accountable in making and maintaining sustainable changes, <u>even after you fall down initially</u>?

YES   NO

If you answered YES to any of these questions, then you are ready to go deeper in the questions you ask to reach your goal.

2. Asking deeper questions requires you to look at places that cause you discomfort. Although this may seem intimidating, being uncomfortable is the beginning of authentic learning. However, years of disappointment in not breaking through the discomfort to find resolution can us to shut down when dealing with these painful memories. To help gently nudge you forward, circle the commitment level you can realistically give. By asking yourself tough questions you move from low level awareness to high level awareness. Assess the commitment you are willing to make in addressing these prickly questions toward realizing your goal. Circle a number representing <u>your willingness</u> to go deeper into your authentic self to "live your questions." DO NOT ANSWER THESE QUESTIONS AT THIS TIME. Just be willing to look at what level of commitment you are willing to give them. *Describing* gives the facts but not the feelings ("I gained 50 pounds after I ended a relationship."). *Clarifying* gives feeling and facts but may veer towards rationalization ("I gained 50 pounds after I ended my last relationship. He was probably right when he said I think like an overweight person."). *Being curious* means looking at the situation nonjudgmentally ("I gained 50 pounds after I ended my last relationship. What's really motivating me to do this?"). Circle a

number from 1 – 5 that best represents your willingness to take a deeper look at yourself.

| DESCRIBING | CLARIFYING | BEING CURIOUS |

a. What causes me to abandon my effort after a disappointment (ex: weight loss, eating right, exercising, making more money, finding a right-fit job, finding a compatible partner, etc.)?

| 1 | 2 | 3 | 4 | 5 |

b. How does this situation mirror an unresolved aspect of myself?

| 1 | 2 | 3 | 4 | 5 |

c. What are my old mental messages or beliefs about this?

| 1 | 2 | 3 | 4 | 5 |

d. What tools will help me with this situation?

| 1 | 2 | 3 | 4 | 5 |

3. Conduct this thought exercise. Look at the horizontal line below. The right end of the line represents your fluid life, your abundant life, your life as you choose it in the present moment from a "both/and" perspective. The left end of the line represents your fixed life with a focus on deficits and limitations, a life of indecision fixated on the past or future. These are symptoms of an *"either/or"* perspective. The solid line is what you

already know; the dotted lines are what's unknown, or of partial memory about the experiences and people you want to attract.

― ― ― ― ― ― ― ― ――――――――― ― ― ― ― ― ― ― ―

a. Place a fulcrum somewhere along the solid horizontal line as a representation of how you view your life unfolding. Be as honest and nonjudgmental as you can. If the fulcrum is not at the midpoint of the horizontal line – a rare event for most of us – ask yourself where you would like it to be.

b. On which side of the fulcrum would you put the following questions:

❖ Am I giving a high priority to self-judgment?

❖ Can I be happy despite my perceived deficits?

❖ Can I quiet my mind when my "hot" button gets pushed?

❖ Do I display victim identity when something does not go my way?

❖ What opportunities lay hidden in the adversity?

❖ Can I trust my instinct about my innate wisdom to pursue a healthy path?

❖ Can I show compassion to my emerging (and fragile) self when I make a mistake?

4. Are you willing to live the life you've imagined? If so, answer these questions that put you in the direction of your dreams:

   a. What happened today that made you keep going to satisfy unmet needs?

   _____

   _____

   _____

   _____

   _____

   b. What did you learn from that? What's your takeaway?

   _____

   _____

   _____

   _____

   c. What surprised you or what mistake did you make that taught you something?

   _____

   _____

   _____

   _____

   _____

d. What strategy are you going to try to get back on track?

_____

_____

_____

_____

5. Now let's have another look at the questions you addressed in number 2. How would answer these questions given an abundant perspective rather than a deficit perspective?

| DEFICIT PERSPECTIVE | ABUNDANT PERSPECTIVE |

a. What causes me to abandon my effort after a disappointment?

_____

_____

_____

_____

_____

b. How does this situation mirror an aspect of myself?

_____

_____

_____

_____

c. What are my old (and new) mental messages or beliefs about this?

_____

_____

_____

_____

_____

d. What tools will help me with this situation?

_____

_____

_____

_____

_____

6. Draw an image of the new YOU reaching your goal. Select an image that is out of the ordinary. Make sure it is affirming your new sense of self. Make sure it is amazing!

Gratitude

This final section is about gratitude. Living a more vibrant life is about letting go of old patterns and beliefs about yourself and formulating new ways of being. Gratitude supports finding blessings in your life. Your life is filled with good deeds that often goes unnoticed. Identifying your gratitude, often in the midst of discomfort, can open your eyes to see the unseen and rich blessings all around. By acknowledging your empathy for yourself and others, you let go of unproductive protections of your ego and allow an emotional self-care to open your heart to the fruits of compassion. By tapping into your grit you let go of hesitation or ambivalence and support perseverance and connection to your passion. By shifting from a fixed mindset to a growth mindset you let go of beliefs which no longer work for you as you move into a new ways of thinking about yourself and your world. Ask the important and hard questions. Face the fear. Feel the gratitude.

[The surface layer]

Every day I am thankful for:

_____

_____

_____

Claim Your Light - Gaining Insight for a Fulfilling Life Workbook

[Digging a little deeper]

Even in my darkest hour I appreciate:

[Breaking through the hard rock protecting past hurts]

When I don't edit or prejudge my motivations, I *know* my new way of life will be:

_____

_____

_____

_____

_____

_____

_____

_____

_____

_____

_____

_____

_____

_____

_____

_____

_____

_____

Biography

Wayne Benenson, Ph.D., has a lot of gypsy energy in him. He has taught in many classrooms, from preschool to grad school, in public and private schools, in 13 different cities. His lifelong quest has been to be available for the teachable moment with whomever and wherever it might show up. He has a keen interest in training school-based peer mediators, coaching for transformational leadership and sensing the feng shui in his office as it extends to the desert view outside the window. In the evening he looks forward to his dog walking him. He can be contacted at wbenenson2700@comcast.net.

Barb Hughson, is the owner and CEO of DurangoLearns, a potpourri of leadership training, nonprofit management courses and continuing education plus practical classes (cooking, spoken Italian, internet graphic design, etc.) led by subject experts from the community. She has used her degrees, a MA and a MS.Ed in Counseling and Education and an Ed.D in Organizational Leadership, to further her passions as a family mediator and children and adolescents therapist. She thoroughly enjoyed her recent incarnation offering faculty training and support at a university in Seattle. She continues working with companies to design and facilitate learning that works for all levels. She can be contacted at CEO@DurangoLearns.com

For further information about our 'Shift' program contact us at wbenenson2700@comcast.net or CEO@DurangoLearns.com.

Go to www.GreatMastersInc.com to join the GreatMasters Tribe and sign up for our great program!

www.ingramcontent.com/pod-product-compliance
Lightning Source LLC
Chambersburg PA
CBHW021136300426
44113CB00006B/457